"Hey Ref, You Stink!"

FINDING YOUR WORTH
IN A WORTHLESS WORLD

by
Marlon G. Sparks

"Hey Ref! You Stink!"
Finding Your Worth in a Worthless World
ISBN: 9781450709958
Copyright © 2018 by
Marlon G. Sparks
P. O. Box 692
Perryton, TX 79070

Photography by: Roger Pasque and Aldena Baker
panhandleillustrated.com
Cover and Text Design: Lisa Simpson
SimpsonProductions.net

For Information Booking Contact:
Marlon Sparks
P.O. Box 692
Perryton, TX 79070
marlongsparks20@gmail.com
806-228-0117

ACKNOWLEDGEMENTS

A special shout out to the men and women in the sports officiating world. You are a very unique group of people. No one but you will ever understand why you do what you do. Your harshest critics would never step in and take your place. There are many times that "you" are the only friend you have, or so it seems. You are not perfect, but people are able to enjoy the thrill of athletics because of YOU!

Thank you!

CONTENTS

INTRODUCTION

The sports officiating world can be wild and crazy. I have been doing it for quite a while. Thirty-five years to be exact. I love telling stores of some of the wilder moments. A few of my friends suggested that I put some of these stories in book form. So here we go!

There is no way that I could ever put all of the stories in a book as they would fill up several volumes. I have tried my best to share a few of the more interesting ones that stand out in my mind. I trust you will enjoy them. Some are funny, some are a little more serious, and some are just downright dangerous!

If you have been around sports at any level for any amount of time at all, you probably have a few referee/umpire stories of your own. It has been a great journey, and I have loved every minute of it. Well, maybe not every minute, but almost!

The names, places, particular schools, times, and dates of each story have been omitted to protect the innocent – ME!

Marlon G. Sparks

CHAPTER 1

IN THE BEGINNING

I t was a beautiful fall Saturday morning. I was at home relaxed, laid back, just chillin', enjoying life, not bothering anyone.

AND THEN . . . THE TELEPHONE RANG

A voice of desperation on the other end of the line shared a problem of heart-stopping magnitude. He was with a group of kids at the YMCA who were waiting to play a basketball game. The problem: They didn't have a referee. He said, "Someone told me you had some refereeing experience, and I was wondering if you could help us out?"

(Note: I'm still looking for the snitch who told him that!)

Now admittedly, it would not be a rookie endeavor. I did have some officiating experience. While attending college, I met Bill Scheer who is now the pastor of Guts Church in Tulsa, Oklahoma. (I know this probably doesn't mean anything to you, but just thought I'd give Bill and his church a plug!)

Anyway, a man had approached him about refereeing some games for a boys' reform school league in the Tulsa area. He asked me if I wanted to help him. As I was pondering my response, he said, "They will pay us to do it!"

Being the typical starving college student needing to make some extra cash, I said, "I'm in!" I thought this could actually be a great opportunity. Besides getting paid, there would be no fans in attendance other than the staff, the place would be crawling with armed guards, and the players would be **forced** (by their unfortunate incarceration) to be on their best behavior. Even though neither Bill nor I had much of an idea what we were doing (from the officiating side of things), hey, the money was money, and we were ready to meet the challenge!

I was still somewhat hesitant, however, to take on this new task of officiating children's league basketball. I had been around sporting events most of my life, playing or spectating, and had seen enough wild, emotional, nasty behavior towards officials from coaches and fans that my inner warning mechanisms were on high alert.

The director did his best to assure me that no "negative behavior" towards me would be tolerated and that he and a number of his staff would be present in case anyone would even have the slightest thought of disrespect. On top of that, he offered to pay me for my effort. Five whole dollars!

Bravely fighting off his incessant pleading (not to mention the opportunity for instant wealth), I respectfully DECLINED!

The words were then spoken that I will never forget as long as I live. The words that to this day I hear in my inner soul. The words that shaped me and helped mold me into the man that I am today. He said, "Mr. Sparks, I don't know if this will have any bearing on your decision or not, but if you don't call these games, THESE KIDS CAN'T PLAY."

I get it! This guy is trying to lay a huge guilt trip on me. He is just trying to emotionally break me down, working on my "soft side." He was attempting to shame me into his little trap!

Whatever he was trying to do, it was working. Just the image of these children clinging to their parents, weeping, being led or even carried to the car was all it took. I could see them heartbroken, completely devastated, and possibly scarred for life because no one cared. And it would all be my fault!

With all of my defensive mechanisms destroyed, all I had left in me was, "What time do I need to be there?"

THE JOURNEY BEGINS!

. . . And remember as we journey, **ALL I WANTED TO DO WAS HELP!**

CHAPTER 2

A LOCAL HERO

It is always a good feeling when you think you are helping someone out of a seemingly hopeless situation. That was the feeling I had on my way to the gym on that fall Saturday morning.

I had the feeling that a superhero must experience while on his way to rescue the "damsel in distress." The feeling that Superman had when he rescued Lois Lane from certain death! The same feeling that Underdog had when he rescued Sweet Polly Purebred from the wretched villain. The same heroic feeling that Mighty Mouse had when he would loudly proclaim in his booming singing voice, "HERE I COME TO SAVE THE DAY." (I dated myself on that one!) Anyway, I think you get it!

I walked into the gym that day and WOW! What a glorious celebration! Cheers, applause, pats on the back, handshakes, and high fives all around. "Thank you, Mr. Sparks. You're awesome! What a great guy! You're so kind!

You'll never know how much we appreciate this!" . . . And on and on and on . . .

I WAS A LOCAL HERO!

My daddy always told me, "Son, go where you are celebrated, not where you are tolerated." I guess I'm in the right place! Could this day get any better? LET'S PLAY BALL!

CHAPTER 3

THE GREAT CHANGE

Now, it would be very difficult, if not impossible, to describe to you the change in the atmosphere that came over the room as the ball went into the air to begin this contest. Within minutes those who had moments earlier hailed me as a hero, a savior, a god in the referee world – TURNED ON ME! I watched and listened in shock and amazement as these people who had just sung my praises began to experience a very ugly transformation.

These people began to voice their extreme displeasure with my officiating expertise. What began as a low murmur was now rising in an ever-resounding, nasty crescendo of rage with every trip down the court.

(Note: Did I leave this part out? These were seven- and eight-year-old girls who were playing in this game!)

"She walked with the ball," some screamed! Yes, they're ALL walking with the ball! (Actually, they were RUN-NING with the ball, but let's not get picky!)

"She double dribbled," they raged! Yes, they're ALL double-dribbling! (These girls didn't know a "legal dribble down the court" from "a messy dribble down their chin"!)

"She pushed her," they angrily complained! Ya think? Of course they were pushing! They were ALL pushing! Even the girls on the same team were pushing EACH OTHER!

"She's grabbing her," one mother loudly yelled as her head spun around in true "exorcist-like" fashion with added flames of fire shooting from her eyes. Yes, lady, I know. At times this game looked like a group hug fest!

Admittedly they were ALL walking with the ball, foul-ing, grabbing, pushing, shoving, and slapping. They were breaking every basketball rule known to mankind.

"I know that James Naismith, the inventor of this great game of basketball, was somewhere spinning in his grave like a Dewalt drill on high speed, thinking, *This is not what I had in mind!"*

There was no real basketball being played here! It was a rugby match in pigtails! It looked like nothing more than a flock of little chicks scurrying about, chasing after the farmer at feeding time, then being the first to dive into the pile to get the first thrown piece of grain. Wherever the ball was, they all gathered and "WOE BE" to whoever got in the way!

Finally, I realized, this game couldn't be officiated. It could only be monitored! The safety and protection of these children was now my only concern. In most parts of the country, these girls would be arrested for assault and battery! To see that there was no loss of life had become my ultimate goal!

But if you were to ask these coaches, fans, and of course, the precious moms about this game, they seriously thought these kids were good! I know that somewhere in their biased (and warped) grip on reality, they just knew that a scout from a major college, or even greater, someone from the WNBA was somewhere in the crowd looking for new talent, and this was their child's opportunity to shine.

Just maybe at the end of the day that scout would approach the family with an incredibly lucrative offer to make their "little sweetie" a child basketball superstar. A multi-year contract, large signing bonus, and worldwide fame were no doubt going to be offered depending on the outcome of this game. I guess it was now partly up to me to make it happen.

Yes, the crowd turned on me that day! They had digressed from singing my praises TO AN ANGRY:

"Hey, ref, you stink!"

"Are you blind?"

"Open your eyes!"

"You're terrible!"

"Where did you guys find this clown?"

"Are you kidding me? That's the worst call I've ever seen!"

"Go home, loser!"

"What a moron!"

And those are just the comments that I can put in print!

But then, the "ULTIMATE!" Just as the game ended and I was doing my best to exit the building in a peaceful manner, a dad of one of the players approached me. He was red faced, veins bulging in his neck, and shaking with anger. He was at least 6'5", 275 lbs. He angrily growled at me, gritting his teeth, and said, "I'll meet YOU in the parking lot, boy, and we ain't goin' out there to chat!"

Needless to say, I was stunned! I was looking around for help, but there seemed to be no help available. (Note: My "pastoral" blood wanted to rise up in me and shout back, "Demons, come out of this man!" But I wisely and fearfully refrained.) I tried my best to ignore him, pushed my way past him, and made my way at a rather hurried pace to my car. He thankfully didn't follow.

I sat in my car, silent for just a moment, collecting my thoughts. "Are you kidding me? Did that all just happen?" You may be asking yourself, "Could all of that really be true?" Yep! All true! (All except that demon part, but I needed a spiritual moment for the book!)

Now, I know most would think, *"That's it for this guy's reffing career. You can stick a fork in him. He's done! How could a person ever subject themselves again to that kind of abuse? He's finished! It's over! Retired after just one game."* WELL, THINK AGAIN!

I know this is going to be very difficult to explain to those "sound in mind." Maybe it was stubbornness. Maybe it was some kind of mentally disturbed male ego determination that no one is going to get the better of me. I don't really know, but I actually began to have serious thoughts about the possibility of doing this ref thing again! It wouldn't be the same crowd ever again, and it couldn't possibly ever be this wild and crazy!

Don't know if I'm calling someone out on a third strike
or defending myself from an angry mom!

CHAPTER 4

MY OFFICIATING CAREER BEGAN THAT DAY

THE KIDS WERE HAVING FUN!

I actually took a positive thought away from this experience – THE KIDS! I remember thinking about the fun they were having. Yes, in the midst of all of this mayhem and chaos, while the parents and coaches were having wild and crazy "out of the body experiences," the kids were having a blast. Watching them have fun seemed to help me block everything else out.

I remember the thrill of watching these kids make their first "real basket," though not all that many points were scored that day. I've never seen greater excitement and joy. The team who scored would stand on one end of the court, jumping up and down, giggling, screaming, hugging, and celebrating with their teammates, while the other team would hurriedly take the ball down the court and try to score before the other team came to their defensive senses. Forget about playing defense for the moment. We made a basket, and it's time to party. The pure joy of a child! Thinking about that made me feel good about my day!

Yes, I got home that afternoon, and these thoughts actually began to go through my mind. *"I wonder if I could do this reffing thing for real? I mean, if I survived (barely) something like that, how much worse could it get? After all, I got great exercise, I got to be personally involved in a game that I love, I enjoyed being around kids having fun, and I got paid (five whole dollars). Maybe if I got into this for real, they might actually pay more money; and I'm quite certain that the behavior and abuse couldn't be any worse."* (Okay, I was wrong about that behavior and abuse thing not getting worse, but . . . Oh, well!)

To make a very long story short, my officiating career of thirty-five years was born that day. I became so wrapped up in this experience that through the years, besides basketball, I added football, baseball, and women's softball to my refereeing/umpiring endeavors. I worked all the way into the collegiate level. I did have some aspirations to go up higher, but my church ministry was my first love. Due to the fact that most of the games are on weekends (and the fact that I do probably stink at it – LOL!), that took care of that.

MOVIN' ON UP!

In the next few days I did make a few phone calls and did a little personal research, and sure enough, it seems as though everyone was looking for officiating help. (Note: There always seems to be a shortage of officials. Hard to believe, I know. Right?) So I joined a "genuine" referee association and started "helping out." I have always tried to carry these words with me throughout my career: "If you don't call the game, these kids can't play." Those words always seemed to keep me motivated and kept me coming back for more!

(Note: Statistically, 79 percent of sports officials will quit after their first year. The reason they give for quitting: Abusive coaches, parents, and fans. I had no idea that I was about to shatter that statistic.)

I was extremely fortunate in my early years to have had several experienced veteran mentors who were willing to take me under their wings and work with me. One of them once told me, "Young man, always remember this: OFFI-CIATING IS KIND OF LIKE BEING MARRIED . . . IF YOU JUST HANG IN THERE FOR A FEW YEARS, YOU LEARN TO DEAL WITH BEING SCREAMED AT AND BERATED ON A DAILY BASIS; AND YOU

STICK WITH IT BECAUSE YOU LOVE THE KIDS." (Note: Not my marital experience, of course. I was just repeating what he said, and I thought it was cute. Honest! No, seriously!)

As for the fans, players, and coaches who would have to be dealt with, let's just say: They pay our local Law Enforcement, S.W.A.T. Teams, Military Personnel, Special Forces, and Navy Seals for a reason. I had great confidence that, if need be, I could trust them to do their job!

Through the years, I have had a few of those "if need be" experiences.

CHAPTER 5

PROTECTING THE FAMILY NAME

I remember the first time my wife attended a high school game that I was officiating. It was a game I had conveniently scheduled en route to visit our parents in central Texas.

She found a seat on the home side of the court, surrounded by the hometown faithful. About four minutes into the game, I noticed she was no longer in her seat. I thought possibly she had gone to the ladies' room or to the concession stand, so I didn't think much about it. She never came back to her seat. I thought maybe she had gone to the car to rest up for our trip as we would be driving through the night. That was not the case.

When I arrived at the car after the game, she was sitting on the passenger's side with her arms folded, and let's just say she did not appear to be too happy. She blurted out in a rather angry tone, "Have you lost your mind? (We had been married a couple of years at that time, so I thought that was evident.) Do you have any idea what those people were saying about you? Could you not hear the names they were calling you?"

I smiled and answered, "Yes, I know. That's just part of it." Then I asked, "Did you say something?" "Of course I did," she said. Then she began to explain to me how she had tried to defend my honor and our family name. Apparently they did not take well to her coming to my defense.

Needless to say, with her being somewhat outnumbered, I truly think she had gone to the car to avoid causing a scene or maybe for her own protection. Or, knowing her, maybe for THEIR protection! I couldn't quit laughing about it. She didn't think it was funny! Fortunately, there were only a couple of other times that she and a fan or two had an altercation.

I had been forced into action once again, due to a shortage of officials, to officiate a JV game that my son Seth was playing in.

Note: For any future official who may be asking, "Is it a good idea to referee your children's ball games?" The answer is "NO!" That's another no-win situation. You're probably going to hear some "constructive criticism" when you get home. My kids and my wife always felt like they were getting the bad end of that deal. They would accuse me of being harder on them because I didn't want to appear biased.

A group of fans from the other team somehow found out who I was and that I had a possible "personal interest" in the outcome of this contest. Then they found out who my wife and daughter were. Somehow, because of the smallness of the gym and the large size of the crowd, many of the two opposing factions had become intermingled on the same side. (Note: Also, never a good idea!)

It was a wildly contested game, and it was now getting "personal." Because of the barrage of insults and character bashing comments that were being hurled their way, simply because of their association with me and the fact that a number of our local fans and visiting fans were about to have a good old-fashioned "throw down," they were forced to pick up their belongings and gingerly move to a much safer area. This was much to the delight (with jeers and applause) of the angry mob.

CHAPTER 6

A FAMILY BUSINESS? NOT!

My boys, Cody and Seth, were pretty good athletes. Whitney, my daughter, was too until she gave it up for cheerleading and beauty pageants . . . Oops! Excuse me! . . . scholarship pageants. I thought maybe they would one day (the boys at least) catch the reffin' bug and follow in my footsteps and go into officiating. However, getting them to call a game was like pulling teeth!

During their college years, occasionally I, or a school somewhere, would get in a jam where emergency referee help was needed. I would do my best to convince them this was the best way to make some fast, "easy" money, which, of course, wasn't exactly true. But they were young, impressionable, and still developing brain cells, so what did they know!

Seth, my youngest, usually had a very easygoing temperament, much like me. He was never wild about calling a game, but he, understanding the nature of sports, would usually take everything in stride and just let the critical comments roll off.

Cody, my oldest, was quite different. His distaste for officiating was very simple. He hated being yelled at. He would help, but there always had to be some kind of special incentive involved. One major thing was, he preferred to work with me as his partner if at all possible. And believe me, I also preferred to be HIS partner for good reason.

More than once while working with him, I would find myself sprinting across the basketball court or football field wildly blowing my whistle in order to break up a nose-to-nose confrontation between he and a disapproving fan or coach. One time he said, "I'm not like you, Dad. I need everyone to like me. You don't really seem to care if they like you or not." (Hey, son, I'm just here to help!)

One particular incident stands out in my mind. Cody and Seth had formed a Texas Country Band – The Cody Sparks Band – and moved to Austin, Texas. I think they were going through a Duck Dynasty stage in their lives, and by their appearance could have easily been part of the television family. They both looked like "wild mountain men"!

Cody had come home for a visit, and it just so happened that a local Junior Varsity Tournament was being played. As fate would have it, we needed referee help. I made my way to his bedroom and told him our situation. He laughed and said, "No way, Dad. I hate reffing, and besides, I don't especially look the part." I laughed too and said, "I suppose it doesn't matter at this point what you look like. We are desperate for help, and you need the money so let's go!"

We quickly threw a uniform together consisting of his old high school red and white basketball shoes and a pair of black shorts. I loaned him a referee shirt and whistle, and he found a white head band to keep his moppy hair out of his eyes. He was a beautiful picture of refereeing excellence.

We started the game, and one of the coaches soon got on Cody's case. His disagreements intensified each time we went up and down the floor. Knowing Cody, I knew an ugly confrontation was inevitable. Suddenly I heard a shrill whistle and heard him address the coach in a resounding, "Coach, that's enough. NOW, SHUT UP!"

The gym was suddenly quiet, and the stunned coach shouted back, "SHUT UP? SHUT UP? You just told me to SHUT UP? Wow! That's real professional!"

Cody took a few steps back so the coach could get a good look at him, and said, "Hey, Coach. Do I look *real professional* to you?" and walked away.

As I was rushing to intervene, I saw the coach put his hand over his mouth and turn away, obviously trying to keep from laughing. He didn't hold it in for very long as he and the players and coaches on the benches from both teams all began to laugh.

As we were leaving the court at halftime, a lady, more than likely a mother of one of the players, leaned over the rail dividing the stands from the court. She screamed angrily at Cody with her booming, southern, red-necked drawl, "Hey, you, Willie! You might make great duck calls, but you ain't made a good basketball call all day." All of those within ear shot found that wildly amusing! But, of course, she didn't think it was funny.

Come on, lady! He's only trying to help! Where's the love?

CHAPTER 7

THE BLAME GAME – TIME TO VENT

I have been asked many times over the years, "Are you a good official/umpire?" Usually I give them the standard answer, "I'm not sure there is such a thing as a *good* official/umpire. It's just that some are better than others." I suppose it depends on who you ask. There are those who think you're the best they have ever seen, and others who wouldn't have you call their game if you were the last official on the earth.

We have all learned that we are just as good as our next "bad call." Any official who puts on the uniform knows that he or she is putting themselves in a "no-win" situation. With every close call, you are going to make someone mad and someone glad.

I'm not sure of the degree of difficulty there is statistically in officiating a sporting event, but I am sure it's right up there with "milking alligators," "juggling lit sticks of dynamite," or "cleaning a rattlesnake pit." No matter how good you are at it, you are eventually going to get bit or something (or someone) is going to blow up. Every official knows going into a game that he or she will more than likely be involved in the "blame game."

Coaches deal with the same problem. People love blaming the coach or officiating. "Our coach is terrible. He's gotta go. Let's get rid of him." The truth is, like an official, that coach never missed a shot, never dropped a pass, never fumbled the ball, never committed an error, etc., but somehow it's his fault. I've heard people make those comments about officials and coaches whether their team lost a game by 50 points or by 1 point.

One coach who had just lost a football game by 58 points felt it necessary to loudly declare his displeasure with our crew. "Bad job, guys. Horrible job," he angrily yelled at us as we made our exit.

One of my buddies yelled back, "Hey, Coach. I know we may be bad, but even this crew isn't 58 points bad." (Usually we don't comment, but I guess he just thought something needed to be said.) I suppose that's just the competitive human nature in all of us. Sometimes we just need a "scapegoat." I've done it myself (sad to say).

Once in a college baseball tournament semifinal game, one particular team was leading by 5 runs going into the last inning. I was calling behind the plate. The team in the lead only had to get 3 outs, and they would be moving on to the championship.

After a few base hits and 3 or 4 horrible errors later, they lost by one run. As the game ended, the losing coach came charging at me with an obvious issue. In his opinion, I had missed "a pitch" that would have given them their third out and the win. "That loss is on you. You're horrible. It's your fault," he screamed at me, nostrils flaring.

I thought to myself, *"Really? What about that easy fly ball your center fielder dropped or that horrible throw by your left fielder? What about your shortstop letting that easy routine ground ball go under his glove and through his legs? Your first baseman dropped an easy, perfect throw that would have ended the game. And it's MY fault?"*

I saw well over 200 pitches in the game, and he said I "maybe" missed one pitch. (Not a bad percentage.)

A basketball coach did the same thing. He came running across the court after the game blaming me and my partner for his one point loss because we counted a shot as a 2-pointer instead of a 3-pointer. (The video clearly showed his player's foot was on the line.) He failed to mention the fact that his players had missed over 20 free throws and several easy basket attempts during the second half of play. Our fault? We report. You decide!

Hey! That's what we do in the officiating world. We will, more often than not, bear the brunt of a close loss so a coach or his team can go free of any blame or personal responsibility. And you know what, though unjust, we learn to deal with it! Feel sorry for us yet? I didn't think so! LOL!

CHARACTER ASSASSINATION

Let me speak a word in the coaches' defense (and please don't let any coaches know I said this . . . another LOL). Anyone involved in athletics, on any level, even pee-wee leagues, realizes that we live in a "win at all cost" world, and the pressure on coaches to win can be overwhelming. Winning is demanded by school administrations and communities, or else. Coffee shop talk is usually, "If we just had a different coach we would be awesome." The team's talent level is seldom taken into consideration.

PERSONAL OPINION: "The pressure to win has led to the anger level of coaches and parents increasing dramatically in the past few years. The berating and verbal abuse being directed toward the players has gotten way out of hand. I believe it's all because of heavy 'win' pressure. Life expectancy has got to be dropping in the coaching world. So let's all sing together: 'Mamas, don't let your babies grow up to be coaches!" (WARNING: "Coaching (and officiating) may be hazardous to your health!)

Admittedly, there is very little appreciation for the job a coach does. I can't imagine having the security and welfare of my family depending on the performance of a bunch of wild, immature, scatter-brained teenagers. Who to play and who not to play can lead to serious issues between a coach and his players and/or parents.

I was told that a basketball coach once put all ten of his players on the court at the beginning of a game. The official told him to take five of them off the floor, and the coach said, "No, we're good." Refusing to comply with the insistence of the referee, the coach was given a technical foul. He then turned to the stands where the parents were seated and addressed them all, saying, "See there parents, I told you I couldn't start all of them at the same time." Lots of pressure!

CHAPTER 8

THE BIBLE, THE BADGE, AND THE YO-YO

I love a good story. My grandfather, Clarence Peterson, was a good ol' Panhandle of Texas wheat farmer. Man, could he tell some stories about the old days! Grandkids and great grandkids would spend a lot of time sitting around on holidays listening to him tell his tales. I actually have a video of him telling my two oldest children (when they were about ages five and three) stories of when he was 19, and his youngest brother was 13, moving from central Oklahoma to the Panhandle of Texas in a covered wagon.

Just think about that! He traveled in a covered wagon and saw men walk on the moon in his lifetime. Amazing how mankind had progressed in such a short time. He passed away at the age of 91.

My dad, Bill Sparks, was the most amazing man I've ever known. What a life he lived! He had a troubled "fatherless" childhood. He left home at the age of 15, moved to Dallas, and immediately fell in with the wrong crowd. He ended up, unknowingly, running black market beef for the Mafia. That didn't end up so well. Fearing for his life, he moved to New Mexico to live with an uncle who just happened to be the pastor of a local church.

Long story short, my dad committed his life to Christ at his uncle's church and had an amazing life transformation. His addiction to alcohol was broken immediately. His fear, despair, and hopelessness were all replaced with an amazing peace that, to quote him, "Only God could have done that." He had found God's "amazing grace." It was truly God's undeserved, unearned, unmerited favor. He knew if God could do that for him, he could do it for anyone.

Note: Sorry to get preachy on you, but that's who I am! WARNING: I get worse later on in the book!

In order to quit smoking after his conversion, he took up the yo-yo. Every time he needed a smoke, he would pull out the yo-yo instead. He got quite good at it through the years, even setting a couple of world records. He made the string extremely long and loved to throw the yo-yo at people to see how close he could come to their nose. The string snapped once when he jokingly threw it towards my mom. It hit her in the head, knocking her out cold. He yo-yoed even into his latter years. He passed away at the age of 80, still yo-yoing.

Soon after his "miracle transformation," he felt a special call into the ministry. He later met my mom at a church campmeeting. They enrolled in the same Bible college (he was probably just chasing her, but he says he went to learn).

After Bible college they got married, and well, here I am! I was raised in the home of a pastor/evangelist. My dad would preach and my mom, my sisters, and I would provide the special singing at our home church and when we traveled. (I'm not sure how "special" it was, but we would sing nonetheless.)

When I was about ten years old, my dad became involved in law enforcement. He continued pastoring the church as well. He would jokingly say, "If I can't get 'em by GRACE, I'll get 'em by the LAW." (You non-church going people probably won't get that, but. . . .)

I said all of that just to talk about loving my dad and granddad's stories. My dad's church and law enforcement stories were amazing as were my granddads. To this day I regret not recording all of them. Their life stories would have made a great movie or a fascinating book. If I were to write a book on my dad's life story, it would be: "The Bible, The Badge, and The Yo-Yo." That's what he was known for.

CHAPTER 9

WAR STORIES OF COACHES AND OFFICIALS

Listening to a group of coaches or fans tell their "war stories" is one of my favorite things to do. Some coaches have talked to me about their threatening phone calls, being confronted by angry parents, or communities urging them to please "move away."

One coach told me that the worst cursing he ever received was from a lady who thought her son should get more playing time on the high school football team. The problem was that her son was about 5'5" and weighed about 120 lbs. He had no talent, no size, no speed or skill. The young man playing ahead of him was 6'3" and 220 lbs. He was an All-Stater! The simple fact that the boy was devastated that he didn't have a starting position had his mom upset to the point of cursing the coach and his dad to the point of wanting to fight him.

The blame for a loss will most likely go to the coach or the official. It doesn't usually go to the kid (or kids) with little or no talent, or to the kid (or kids) who played a miserable game full of miscues and blunders.

At times there are those in the crowd, and occasionally a coach or player, who choose to associate an official's "poor officiating performance" (their opinion, of course) with that particular official or coach's personal character. That's probably the most difficult issue to handle.

At various places I have been in conversation or overheard someone say when a particular official or coach's name would come up, "Oh, that guy is such a jerk!" or "I can't stand that guy" or worse, "I hate that guy." All of that because there was a disagreement pertaining to a particular call or decision made in a sporting event. I have had close officiating buddies and coaches who have given up on sports or retired way too early because of lost friendships due to a bad call or a bad decision.

In reality, all of these guys and gals are GREAT people. They are hard working, family oriented, civic minded, patriotic, church going, God-fearing, lovable people just trying to help. Hmmm. Okay, not all, but MOST . . .

well, some . . . maybe a selected few . . . all right then . . . ME. I'll just speak for myself!

I'm truly a nice guy. I'm the nicest person I know. It's just so hard for me to imagine anyone not personally liking me because of a (in their opinion) missed call. I'm very cute, kind, and loveable. Just ask my wife! Okay, on second thought, maybe you should ask my kids. All right then, maybe you should ask my mom. She likes me!

But you know, it doesn't matter how nice of a person we are or attempt to be, all officials miss calls and all coaches make poor decisions. The power of being able to separate "the man or woman" from his or her officiating or coaching performance on the court or field is something that I guess we will be working on until the end of time.

Believe me, it takes real "character" not to respond back when names and/or insults are being hurled at you from total strangers, and you have to "professionally" turn a deaf ear to it. An official who has, as we affectionately call it in the officiating world, "rabbit ears," usually doesn't last long.

An angry young official once told me, "I don't have to take that kind of abuse." I assured him that if he wanted to continue in this profession that he actually *did* have to take it (to a certain degree) and if he couldn't, then he needed to retire early. Thankfully, for his sake he did!

The most frequent adjectives used to describe an official's performance from the stands or the sidelines that you can hear throughout the game are: "That's horrible," "That's terrible," or "That's pathetic!" Personalizing it is probably the most difficult criticism.

The bad call doesn't make the official a "terrible, horrible, or pathetic" person. It was just (and possibly was) a terrible call. It happens! It is sad, however, when people can hold personal grudges for a lifetime over human error. That's one of the life lessons, failed by many, in the athletic world: personal character.

I was once involved with three others on a referee crew in a very closely contested Little League football game. One of the coaches was violently protesting a ruling on the field. Our explanation of the ruling did not suffice (although we were correct). They lost and said that "one call" had cost them the championship!

After the game, some of the coaches and a few of the parents marched the team of third and fourth graders over to where my crew and I were resting, getting ready for the next game. The head coach pointed at us and said to the children, "Guys, take a good look. I want you to see what 'real cheaters' look like. These men took the game away from you. You didn't lose the game. These guys stole it from you. These refs are cheaters." (Other things were said by some of the parents that can't be mentioned in this G-rated book.)

The next day that coach, after a number of inquiries, found out that, sure enough, we were right on the ruling. He called me to offer his apology which I accepted. However, the damage was done. For his players and their parents, the integrity of the game and the lesson of sportsmanship and good character were lost.

Okay, let's move on!

No matter how tense the action is there's always
time for autographs!

CHAPTER 10

LOSING CONTROL

If you have not been involved in sports, this book and the stories I am sharing may make little sense to you. But if you are involved and have been around athletics for any amount of time, you get it. You probably have some great stories of your own.

Maybe you have heard about, you have witnessed personally, or you have seen a few television or YouTube video clips of crazy, emotionally charged tirades at an athletic event. Situations that escalated to an emotional, high-fevered pitch, and then someone "popped a cork" and "lost it."

Something like a baseball coach kicking dirt on an umpire or throwing a base while disputing a call. You may have seen a baseball player throwing bats and helmets out of the dugout onto the playing field, angry about a strike-out call. You possibly have watched a nationally televised college basketball game where a coach threw a chair across the court during a disagreement with an official's call.

Several years ago there was a disgruntled coach who followed us to our dressing room. He was cursing at us while kicking our dressing room door and had to be tackled and restrained by a couple of the school board members. He was fired the next day.

Then, there were seven or eight fans at a 7th grade "B-Team" girls' game who had to be removed from the gym for their unruly behavior and unacceptable language. The last one to leave shouted out a verbal threat of physical violence against me and my partner. A local deputy sheriff met him at the top of the stairs, inquiring as to his "terroristic threat" against us.

The man physically pushed the officer out of his way, informing the Deputy that this was none of his business. The officer grabbed him and slammed him into the wall, handcuffing him and forcing him outside and off to jail. (Okay, I hate to celebrate anyone's misfortune, but I rather enjoyed that one! LOL!)

The wildest situation in which I was personally involved happened at a high school basketball game. The two schools were very close in proximity to one another. When that is the case, there usually is the possibility for some "high energy" interaction. Rivalry games are always the breeding ground for the competitive spirit to bring out the best or worst in those involved.

Several hundred people representing each school were in attendance. The place was completely packed, standing room only. Stage bands were playing and cheerleaders were already working hard to get their respective fans worked up into a frenzy for a great game. The noise was deafening. I don't believe I have ever been involved in a more intense "pregame" competitive environment whether it be college or high school. These two schools did not care much for each other, and it was about to become evident.

My partner and I were in our normal pregame position standing at the center stripe directly across from the scorer's table. We were watching the ladies go through their pregame warm-ups. It was then that we heard a rough, angry male voice yelling in our direction from the other side of the gym.

I asked my partner, "Is that guy screaming at us?" He smiled and answered, "I think he is. Have you ever been yelled at during pregame warm-ups, Marlon?" he asked me. "I don't believe I have," I joked. He agreed that this was a first for him as well.

This man was indeed yelling at us (though most of what he said was unintelligible, and the noise in the gym made it even more difficult to comprehend.) Seriously?

He was yelling at the referees, and the game hadn't even started yet! This can't be a good sign.

We came over to greet the coaches and the captains for our pregame meeting. The coach of the team that this man was obviously in favor of asked us to please not allow the actions of this man to influence us negatively in any way towards her team. She said, "This man's daughter is one of my best players, and though he means well, he can be a little overbearing. (A little? I'd hate to see a lot!) We assured her that would not happen.

The game began, and it wasn't long before the action became quite heated. Lots of pushing and shoving and a little "trash talking." In situations like this, we usually try to use verbal warnings, talking our way out of trouble, hoping that will calm things down a bit before we step in and take harsher measures. Sometimes it helps, and sometimes it doesn't.

It was about the middle of the second quarter of play when our "catastrophe" happened.

One of the players had stolen the ball and was on her way down the court to shoot an easy layup. She was followed closely by one of her opponents who apparently didn't take kindly to her stealing the ball from her. As the young lady went up to shoot the ball, the defender went low and took her legs out from under her, causing her to turn a complete flip. The shooter went high into the air and came down with a resounding "thud," flat on her face.

I was following the play and was the first to get to her, knowing that she had to be hurt. Man, was I right. As I got there, she was lying motionless on the floor. Immediately I noticed a pool of dark red blood coming from underneath her head. I frantically began to blow my whistle and summons the coaches, or anyone for that matter, for help.

As they were on their way to render aid to her, she groaned and rolled over slightly. She moved just enough for me to see that not only was her head split, but her arm was broken. It was completely snapped in half. The worst injury, by far, that I had seen or have ever seen to this day (and I have seen many in various sports).

The crowd sat for a moment in stunned silence. Suddenly, the silence was shattered. We heard the voice of our "pregame friend" screaming out with anger. "Hey, ref. She better not be hurt. If she is, I'm going to kick (well, you know) . . ." Yes, unfortunately, it was his daughter lying there on the floor.

He made his way down the steps and onto the court cursing wildly. He was blaming me and my partner for his daughter's injuries. (Never once did he make an attempt to check on his daughter.) Our fault? How could that be our fault? How did we hurt her? We never touched her.

I remember a time when a young lady was knocked to the floor with the breath knocked out of her. Her mother came down from the stands to check on her. After she saw that her daughter was okay, she came at me with her purse, blaming me for her daughter's injury. Mama didn't get to see the end of that game. She was escorted to her car.

I once told a coach that I was going to start wearing a disclaimer notice around my neck that said, "NOT RESPONSIBLE FOR ACCIDENTS." I said, "Coach, if a player wants to give his opponent a Bruce Lee karate kick to the throat, all I can do is call a flagrant foul and throw the kid out of the game. I can't stop the kick."

To this day, it seems whenever a player is hurt, there is always someone in the stands yelling, "Way to go, ref!" I never have understood that, but, oh well, just another part of it, I guess.

This particular night it seems my partner wasn't in the mood to be blamed for hurting a child, so he lost his cool just a little and went after this guy. I managed to pull him away about the same time that two or three men arrived to intercept this angry dad's advance. They drug him, cursing, kicking, and screaming, out the door and into the foyer.

It appeared, however, that before this man was forced to leave the court area, he had passed his anger on to the rest of his fan base. Several hundred fans were screaming at us, blaming us for the young girl's injuries.

I now know how a fallen gladiator felt when the Roman throngs in the Coliseum would spew their displeasure and give the proverbial "thumbs down" gesture to end his life. I don't know about my partner so much, but I was looking around for a close exit door just in case they all rushed the court at once. These people were mad and seeking vengeance.

While waiting for the ambulance to arrive, I noticed that several law enforcement officers were now gathering throughout the building. I was hoping they were called in to bring a little civility to our situation and not called in to arrest me and my buddy for some kind of trumped up "ref abuse" or "impersonating a ref" charge.

It seemed as though the matter had calmed somewhat when we heard a loud commotion coming from the foyer area. Sure enough, our "friend" had broken loose from the authorities and was on his way once again to deal with us. By now, I had had enough of this whole thing and decided to spring into defense mode for the purpose of protecting our good name. It was now my partner's turn to restrain me, which he did and I am thankful.

Eventually the entire mess was cleaned up, and we had to think about restarting the game. I don't think anyone wanted to play basketball after a scene such as that, but as they say, "The show (game) must go on."

We gathered the coaches together once again and laid down some very strict, no tolerance policies before we could continue. All went well the rest of the game. I'm sure, mostly because of the heavy law enforcement presence which was now in the building.

We still had the boys' game to play. We laid down the same no-tolerance policies for them and were able to conclude the evening without further incident.

As we were running off the court at the end of the game, I noticed several people blocking our exit from the gym floor leading to our dressing room. They had formed what appeared to be a "GAUNTLET." Don't know what this is? Let me give you Webster's definition. *GAUNTLET:* "A double file of men (and in this case, men and women) facing each other and armed with clubs and other weapons with which to strike at an individual who is made to run between them."

There were a number of coaches, administration, and law enforcement attempting to hold them back so we could make it to our dressing room safely.

The athletic director was awaiting our arrival in the locker room. He quickly asked, "Where are you guys parked?" I said, "We are parked in the lot in front of the main building." He went further, "What are you driving? I'll need your keys. There are quite a number of displeased people waiting for you to come outside to the parking area. I'll go get your vehicle and bring it around back to a private exit area."

He then gave us instructions on how to get out of town without being spotted. Something like, "Go around this certain building; you will pass a red fence. Go past a blue dog house, turning right here and a left there until you come to a dirt road which will take you back to the main highway."

We followed his directions, and sure enough, we came to the highway. Before we were able to make the turn and begin our journey home, we had to stop and wait for a long procession of about twenty cars traveling at a high rate of speed, going in the same direction we had to travel. No doubt about it, they were looking for us. We simply waited for the last car to go by and then turned, pulling in behind the last car.

After five miles or so, the line of cars had turned around, headed back the way they came, giving up hope of catching their prey. We journeyed on home, a little shaken, trying to find the humor in our situation. We were happy to be alive. "Come on, people. We just wanted to help! LOL!"

When I arrived home, my wife said that I needed to return a call to the president of our referee association. Obviously, he had heard about the incident and wanted a personal report from me and my partner.

He seemed satisfied with my story and then gave me some not so welcome news. He said, "Do you know you have this team (the one with the wounded player) again next week?" to which I replied, "If that is the case, I'm sure you can switch me with someone else."

Fortunately, it again would not be a home game for this bunch but another away game. He said he would try, but there was a huge shortage of officials as a severe flu bug was going around and several had to call in sick. They were having trouble finding enough officials to fill all of the games in the area.

I asked him to do his best not to put me back in a harm's way situation. I told him how the crowd for some reason was apparently blaming us for the injury to the young lady, and I'm sure the offended team (city) would not welcome me back into their presence with open arms.

Note: Coaches always have the option to "scratch" (refuse) an official that they would rather not see for a while. Come on, coach. Now would be a good time to "scratch."

A couple of days went by when I received the call from the secretary of our association informing me that they had depleted all of their referee resources and I would indeed be going to do the game. Both coaches had said there was no problem in me doing the game and both had actually requested that I do it. He then gave me what he assumed would be words of comfort.

Just to be safe, they had laid down a few new "ground rules" for this particular game that should guarantee my safety. Please try to imagine all of the "warm fuzzies" going through me as he told me the following:

1. Do not arrive at the game too early.

2. Do not use the usual referee entrance as a more secluded entrance would be provided. An armed officer will meet you there.

3. Do not come out of your dressing room for pre-game warm-ups.

4. Do not conduct a coaches'/captains' meeting.

5. Only come out of the dressing room when it's time for the game to start. Walk immediately to center court and start the game.

6. There will be a heavy law enforcement presence at the game.

7. And my favorite: GOOD LUCK!

Note: Indeed there were local officers as well as others from three surrounding counties in the building that night. I found out later there were eighteen officers (that we know of) in attendance, some in uniform and some in plain clothes. Nine on each side of the gymnasium placed strategically throughout the stands. They were ordered that if anyone was to get the least bit aggressive in any way, they were to take action and immediately remove them. Each school's coaches, players, and fans had been prewarned to be on their best behavior.

As you can probably guess, that particular game went off without any disturbances, though I must say that I wasn't that thrilled with the attention solely directed at me.

I would catch myself throughout the evening looking for "snipers" in the rafters.

Come on, people. It's a game. It can't be this difficult. Where's the love? I just wanted to help!

CHAPTER 11

#REFFINREV

It's very difficult at times to keep who I am separate from what I do. I "do" officiating. I "am" a minister. I have been pastor of a church since February 14, 1982. I often travel as well, speaking for various church groups, men's events, or sporting venues. Occasionally, one occupation will bleed over into the other, but fortunately, not that often.

One such incident did occur during a baseball game. The game was very close, and the crowd was really getting into the excitement of it all.

Many baseball stadiums, especially at high schools, have an area behind the backstop, usually in front of the first row of bleachers or down the baselines for people to place their comfortable folding chairs. That puts those fans quite close to the action so any comment that is made can be easily heard by the coaches, players, or umpires.

It often seems that certain towns have a "designated" complaint person or persons in nearly every sport. This person or persons make it their sole purpose to stir up the crowd by their comments made toward the coach, a player, or umpire/official. This person or group of people never seem to be content with any decision that is made by the coach or referee/umpire. That was the case in this particular game.

One horribly obnoxious man had made it his sole purpose on this day to make me, the coaches, players, and everyone around him miserable. He would pace back and forth in front of the stands like a caged tiger. He seemed to have a negative comment on every pitch thrown and every play made out in the field. He also ridiculed every coaching decision. His voice was angry and at times seemed almost threatening. Nothing made him happy, and on this particular day, he wasn't making me especially happy either.

I will admit, my tolerance level is higher than most. A couple of times a year, we will have an official "evaluator" sitting in the stands taking notes on our performance. They will jot down their constructive criticisms and/or compliments and mail them out to us a few days later.

A couple of times, especially in basketball, my critiques have been (Hey Ref, you stink! Just kidding!), "You are too tolerant," or "You should have given that coach or player a technical foul or at least a warning for his attitude and actions on the court." Believe me, if a coach or player received a technical foul from me, they deserved it.

Note: I have never *personally* thrown a player or coach out of a game. I have, however, been involved in games where coaches and players have been thrown out, but it was always my intolerant, touchy, mean-spirited partner who did it, not me – LOL! Now as for asking fans to leave a little prematurely, that's a different story. Even then, it has only been a handful of times. You can't always live by the old adage of, "They paid their dollar so let them holler." That too has its limitations.

This was one of those days that I was being pushed to that limit. I was letting this man get "under my skin" and my proverbial "cork" was about to pop. His comments were now becoming extremely obnoxious and personal. He was addressing the crowd in the stands in "speech-like" fashion as to my character and intelligence (or lack thereof). He was speaking loudly enough for me to hear every word.

Note: Three things will get a coach, player, or fan in trouble with me:

1. Accuse me of being personally responsible for a player being injured. (I refer you to the last chapter.)

2. Accuse me of cheating.

3. Make a personal threat.

I could now hear this man making accusations and saying things that were about to get him in a heap of trouble. He was now venturing into an arena with me where few people had gone before.

I had turned around a couple of times, giving him a "warning glare" to get his attention. I would do that until he looked my way. I would shake my head "no" and put my hand up as a warning to stop it.

He was shouting the typical, "You're terrible, you're horrible, or you're pathetic" kind of stuff, but that's just "hate the ref 101 language." That to me is drab and boring. There is no creativity at all in that kind of jargon, but that is about to change.

I heard him loudly proclaim, "Hey, everybody! I don't know that much about this umpire, but somebody said he's supposed to be some kind of a preacher or something like that. I hope he preaches better than he calls a baseball game. Come on, preacher. Give us a sermon. Hopefully it will be better than what you've been giving us so far in this game." He and his small band of followers thought that was funny. I didn't!

Note: Usually, I try to have a quiet, personal, peaceful time of prayer before any game that I work. I ask for things like peace, calmness, patience, kindness, loving my enemies, etc. You know, just simple personal character things.

I once had a young rookie partner who noticed my prayer routine. He shockingly asked, "Man, do you mean to tell me that you pray before you go do a game?" I responded, "Man, do you mean to tell me that you don't! Boy, you've got a lot to learn!"

I guess my prayer time should have been more intense and sincere. My gifts of "calm, longsuffering, and patience" had reached their limits. I had just simply had enough of this guy. I yelled, "TIME OUT," angrily yanked my mask off, turned around and began walking towards this guy with a rage I don't think I had ever experienced in my officiating career. I shouted, "Hey, man. Do you seriously want me to preach you a sermon? REALLY, do you want to hear one?" He (though shocked) mockingly replied, "Hallelujah, Brother! Give us a good one!"

I summoned up the best hellfire and brimstone sermon tone I could muster and with the fervor of John the Baptist or the Prophet Elijah, I screamed, "Okay, man. Here it is. FROM THE BOOK OF FIRST UMPIRE, CHAPTER FOUR, VERSE 12: ARISE, TAKE UP YOUR FOLD-ING CHAIR AND WALK, 'CAUSE YOU'RE OUTTA HERE!'" Of course, I gave it the added touch of a beautiful baseball umpire ejection gesture.

The entire place sat in stunned silence for a moment. Actually I think I had shocked myself as well. With wide eyes he just stood there staring at me. He finally broke the silence with, "Dude, are you serious?" I said, "Absolutely. I have had enough of you and your attitude. Now leave, right now!"

With a hollow-eyed look of disbelief, he slowly walked over, folded up his chair, and quietly exited the confines of the stadium without uttering another word. No one was saying anything. I'm quite sure it was for fear they would be next.

I guess I had put the "fear of God" into everyone present for at least a short moment of time on that day. I was so rattled that I didn't even know how to continue the game. I finally announced (attempting to bring a little levity and civility back into the situation), "Now, before we are dismissed, ushers, will you prepare to receive the afternoon tithes and offerings?" Then, I forcefully put my mask back on, walked towards home plate, and shouted, "NOW, PLAY BALL!"

Well, if I needed to break the ice, I guess I had accomplished it. Those who loved me and even those who had issues with me were beginning to find humor in the moment. Like a giant wave, beginning small, then swelling with every turn as it got closer and closer to the shoreline, the laughter began.

The coach in the third base coaching box was literally down on his knees, laughing hysterically. Players and coaches in both dugouts were laughing. Many of the fans were applauding my "Shakespearian" performance.

The young man who was coming up to the plate would step into the batter's box and then take a step back out of the box because he was unable to gain his composure. I began to wonder if we would ever be able to continue.

Eventually we did resume normal play and got the game completed. A number of years have gone by, and I still hear about that incident. It has followed me around like a bad habit. I even heard someone relating this story to a group of coaches during a "Did you hear this one" moment, not even knowing that I was the one involved.

I HAVEN'T PREACHED AT A GAME SINCE. Let the Church say, "AMEN!"

COLLEGE SPORTS

College sports always take it up a notch in intensity, and I do understand that. The pressure on players to perform well and coaches to win is tremendous. For a coach, it's WIN, you're hired; LOSE, you're fired! Knowing a coach's job is often on the line, both in high school and college, can make this very serious business.

One baseball game I had was being played between a secular university and a Christian university. Both teams were not having especially good seasons. They both desperately wanted to win this particular game.

I won't drag this out with a lot of unnecessary details but I'll just say that the Christian university lost the game by one run on what the coach thought were some very questionable balls and strike calls by my partner and a very close play that went against him in the field, called by me.

The coach let us know in no uncertain terms during the latter part of the game, and as we left the field, what he thought of us as umpires, men, and human beings.

The next day, however, I received an e-mail from him with a very heartfelt Christian apology as to his actions during the game. He felt he had truly overreacted and had said things that he now deeply regretted.

He expressed that he had given his life to Jesus Christ a number of years earlier, and his actions in no way reflected Christ-like character. He hoped this incident would not lead to hard feelings down the road. At the end of his e-mail, he posted several powerful Bible scriptures pertaining to Christian character.

He had no idea I was a minister.

I responded something like this (paraphrasing):

Dear Coach:

In no way would I ever let a situation like this lead to hard feelings as I learned long ago not to carry grudges. I try to understand the pressure of the moment. I also try to take into consideration the pressure to win that you and other college coaches are under.

I do appreciate your kind e-mail and especially the scripture references at the end of your message. I too have committed my life to Christ and endeavor to conduct my life in a way that gives glory to Him.

One particular scripture that I (especially in this profession) pray and declare over myself on a continual basis is found in Matthew 12:22, which says that a blind man was brought to Jesus and He healed him. Coach, that verse has not yet fully manifested in my life, but I am still believing for a complete and total manifestation. Please continue to pray and agree with me for my miracle.

In Christ and in Baseball,
Marlon

Note: Rumor has it that this particular e-mail has made its way around to several different places in the sports world.

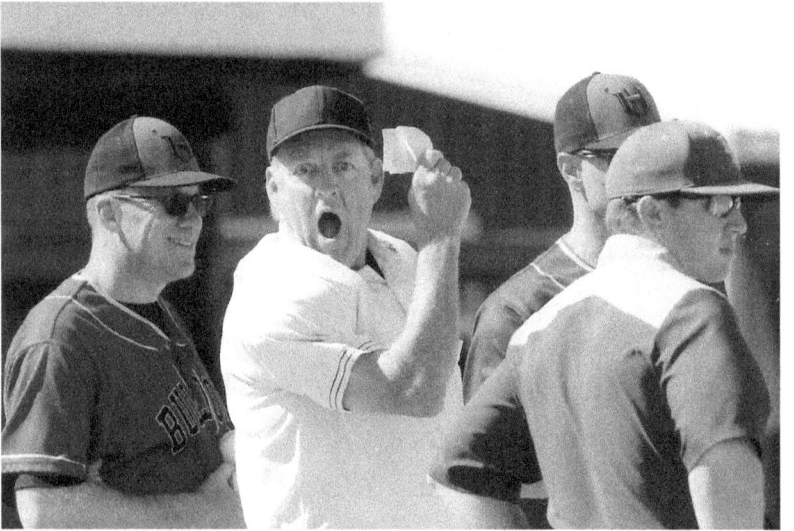

It's shocking what some of these coaches say
about me on their lineup card!

CHAPTER 12

THE BEAUTIFUL WORLD OF THE CREATIVE SPORTS INSULTS

Sporting events are supposed to be fun. Remember, it's a GAME! Many times that thought gets lost in the wild world of spirited competition. Sometimes I enjoy going to a game where I have no favorite team involved in the action. I don't go to watch the game. I go to watch the fans. It is sometimes more entertaining than the game itself. I take notes. I am amazed how the bias towards any one team can completely cloud a spectator's judgment.

In this "sports official" business, you can't help but hear the mean-spirited, angry, personal comments that many will use. The reasons are varied as to why people respond that way. Sometimes the reason is the ref blew the call (and it happens). Other times it's simply a matter of not knowing a particular rule, the game itself, or it's just stupidity! How do I know? Because I've been "ignorant" and "stupid" occasionally myself. Hey, I watched my kids play ball growing up too. I sometimes look back with a little sheepish grin and wonder how we survived it all.

But then there is the artful, creative, fun loving sports fan who will keep the entertainment flowing with a colorful barrage of humorous insults.

I have been asked numerous times what some of the best one-liners are that I have heard coming from the stands. In baseball the umpire is known as "BLUE." So keep that in mind as you read through these. Some of these also cross over into other sports. These are just a "few" of my favorites. (Note: These are somewhat more prevalent in the college games.)

BLUE, UMP, or REF:

We found your cell phone; you've missed four calls.

Is your rule book written in Braille?

Hey, Blue. How can you sleep with all these lights on?

You need to go to confession after that call.

How about some Windex for that glass eye?

I've seen better Blues in a box of crayons.

We know you're blind; we've seen your wife. (Note: She didn't think that one was funny!)

Did your glass eye fog up?

Why do you keep looking in your left hand, Blue? You have a map of the strike zone in it?

It's okay. I was confused the first time I saw a game too.

Can I pet your Seeing Eye dog after the game?

Another call like that, and I'm gonna break your cane and shoot your dog.

Kick your dog, Blue. He lied to ya on that one!

Be careful when you take a step back, Blue. You'll trip over your dog.

I thought only horses slept standing up.

Which one of you is the designated driver?

You can go home. We'll take it from here.

Hey, Blue. What were you? A lookout on the Titanic?

Don't donate your eyes to science; they don't want 'em.

Sure you don't want to phone a friend on that one?

Do you get any better, or is this it?

If the pitcher is throwing too fast for ya, we can ask him to slow down.

Punch a hole in that mask, Blue. You're missing a great game.

You're calling a worse game than a NFL ref. (Note: OUCH!)

Hey, Blue. Now I understand why you and the other manager look so much alike.

Go sit down, bus driver.

You flipping coins?

Is that your final answer?

Turn the plate over, Blue. The directions are on the other side.

Lenscrafter called. They'll be ready in 30 minutes.

When calling in Texas, the chant from the crowd: "T-S-O" (Texas State Optical).

Coach: "Hey, ref. Can you give me a technical foul for what I'm thinking?"

Ref: "Of course not!"

Coach: "Good, cause I think you suck!" (Sorry, Mom.)

Result: He got one! LOL!

. . . and the list goes on and on and on. . . .

CHAPTER 13

GOD SEES YOU AS A PRICELESS TREASURE

A sports official knows going into a contest that he or she must make a predetermined effort to block out all of the negatives being hurled in his or her direction. To allow verbal insults and abusive behavior from coaches, players, or fans to enter into the mind and take root will only lead to poor performance.

I have always found the officiating profession to be a great opportunity to dig deep inside of myself and pull up positive forces of resistance against all demeaning actions and behavior. It has truly been a great life lesson. In officiating (or basic life in general) there is the constant struggle to stay positive and emotionally strong when the odds are definitely not in your favor.

In Christian ministry I deal with people on a continual basis who have had the "joy of living" knocked out of them. The forces of hopelessness and despair are wildly prevalent in today's society, especially in our youth. I don't know anyone who is not facing the barrage of mental trash that's being fed to them daily. We have all been "set up" by this natural life to be run over and demoralized. That just seems to be the negative power of a fallen world. Self-hatred is commonplace. Suicide is becoming an epidemic.

To have a positive, optimistic outlook on life by no means comes naturally. We never had to teach our children to do bad things. Those things just seemed to happen naturally. If we had a dollar for every time we had to say, "NO" – Wow . . . $$$$!

Every parent knows that "good" must be taught to a child through repetitive, diligent, positive reinforcement. To teach a child proper behavior is something done "on purpose" and doesn't happen "by accident." Don't believe it? Just leave your children alone to tend for themselves and see what the end result will be. Note: Are you someone who is discouraged by how your children have turned out? Well, take heart. God is not finished with them. They're still turning!

OUR FATHER WHO ART IN HEAVEN

Many people are surprised when I tell them that I find the most powerful, positive reinforcement material, at least for me, is in the Bible. I mean, after all, we know that through the power of the "New Birth" we are made children of God. Note: That particular opportunity has been made available to everyone, but not everyone will take advantage of it. The decision to accept Christ makes God our "Heavenly Father" by virtue of the new birth according to John 3:3. He is surely Someone who has great parenting skills.

Note: If you are a discouraged parent feeling as though you've failed and "lost" your kids, God knows how you feel. He "lost" His kids for a while too! He had to send Jesus to find them and bring them home.

We can see one of those skills borne out when His only Son, Jesus, was about to begin His earthly ministry. Follow this account in Matthew 3:16-17:

"And Jesus, when he was baptized, went up straightway out of the water: and, lo, the heavens were opened unto him, and he saw the Spirit of God descending like a dove, and lighting upon him:

"And lo a voice from heaven, saying, This is my beloved Son, in whom I am well pleased."

What a powerful moment! Jesus has just received a beautiful affirmation from His Father. Now, please pay close attention to this part because it could possibly have a great effect on you personally. Notice the words of His Father: **"This is my beloved Son, in whom I am well pleased."** My question is this: He is pleased with Him (Jesus) for what? He had yet to do anything notable. He had not performed one single miracle. His ministry was just being launched, yet His Father was pleased with Him.

God was not pleased with Jesus because of something He had done, but He was pleased with Him simply based upon "who He was." Just the fact that Jesus was His Son pleased Him. Now that is real love! With that affirmation of "My beloved Son" firmly tucked away inside of Him, Jesus was now able to go out and confidently "DO" His ministry.

As this story continues into Matthew, chapter 4, we notice this divine affirmation is about to be challenged:

"Then was Jesus led up of the Spirit into the wilderness to be tempted of the devil.

"And when he had fasted forty days and forty nights, he was afterward an hungred. (Don't you just love the *King James Version?* – **He was afterward an hungred.** That's awesome! LOL!)

"And when the tempter came to him, he said, If thou be the Son of God, command that these stones be made bread.

"But he answered and said, It is written, Man shall not live by bread alone, but by every word that proceedeth out of the mouth of God."

Matthew 4:1-4

After that beautiful, powerful, positive Fatherly affirmation, Jesus is met head-on by His enemy (and ours), the devil. You will notice that the devil did not attack Jesus physically. He came after His soul. (Note: Man is a three-part being: spirit, soul, and body. Our spirit IS saved, our soul IS BEING saved, and one day our body WILL BE saved.)

The soul is comprised of the mind, will, and emotions. That will always be the first area of your enemy's attack. If the adversary can win the "battle of the mind," he will arise victorious over you. The Word of God continually reminds us to guard our mind.

Proverbs 4:23 AMP says, **"Keep and guard your heart [mind] with all vigilance and above all that you guard, for out of it flow the springs of life."**

Proverbs 23:7 says, **"For as he** [a man] **thinketh in his heart (mind), so is he. . . ."**

Romans 12:2 states, **"And be not conformed to this world: but be ye TRANSFORMED by the renewing of your mind . . ."** [emphasis mine].

Second Corinthians 10:4-5 AMP says:

"For the weapons of our warfare are not physical [weapons of flesh and blood], but they are mighty before God for the overthrow and destruction of strongholds,

"[Inasmuch as we] refute arguments and theories and reasonings and every proud and lofty thing that sets itself up against the [true] knowledge of God; and we lead every thought and purpose away captive into the obedience of Christ (the Messiah, the Anointed One)."

Third John 2 says, **"Beloved, I wish** (pray) **above all things that thou mayest prosper and be in health, even as thy soul** (mind) **prospereth."** (One translation says, "I pray that you may prosper in every area of your life . . . in direct proportion to the prosperity of your soul (mind, will, and emotions).")

What is a prosperous soul?

1. The mind renewed. (Thinking like God thinks.)
2. The will conformed to the will of God. (Making new, godly choices.)

3. The emotions under control. (Finding promises from God that cover your particular need. God's promises produce peace and destroy fear, worry, and doubt.)

What makes the soul prosperous? Coming into agreement with a new identity in God's Word. Having a confidence in who God says you are. A decision must be made to let go of certain "tags" that this world places on you; things like, "loser," "you're no good," "you're worthless," "you'll never amount to anything," etc. That's exactly what Jesus did in His counterattack.

Notice the mental assault that the devil brought against Jesus in Matthew 4:3: **"If thou be the Son of God. . . ."** The first thing satan did was challenge His sonship. Sound familiar? Have you ever had your position as a child of God challenged? Have you ever had words come up in your mind like, "If you were a real Christian, you wouldn't have done that"? How about, "If you were truly a Christian, you wouldn't have said that"? Satan specializes in sowing seeds of doubt. He is known as the "accuser of the brethren."

How did Jesus pass the test? He boldly looked the devil in the eye and declared, "It is written!" He responded with, "God has said."

Not only did he try to get Jesus to deny His sonship, he then came at Him with a very common weapon, a weapon that I have had the devil use on me personally and no doubt on every person who has ever proclaimed the name of Christ.

Jesus' Father (God) didn't just say, "This is my Son," He said, **"This is my BELOVED Son."** Did you notice that the devil left out that one powerful word, "BELOVED"? Have you ever had the thought, *"God doesn't love me"?* That is without a doubt the biggest lie that has ever been propagated upon humankind.

The devil and "religion" are always trying to make the love of God for you conditional. Did you also notice that the devil said, "If you are the Son of God, DO THIS"? He tried to make His sonship performance-based. But Jesus had already been affirmed as the Son of God before He ever performed anything at all. God loves you based on what Jesus did for you. It is not based on what you did for Jesus. God loves you unconditionally! Embrace that, cling to that, never let it go!

Jesus had a great comeback for the devil when told to **"Command that these stones be made bread** (to prove your sonship)"** (Matthew 4:3). Jesus said, **"It is written, Man shall not live by bread alone, but by every word that proceedeth out of the mouth of God"** (v. 4). Question: What was the word that had just proceeded from the mouth of God? Answer: **"This is my beloved Son, in whom I am well pleased"** (Matthew 3:17). Jesus said, "Man shall LIVE by that powerful word of affirmation." That's how we succeed in this thing called life: knowing that God loves us as His beloved children unconditionally!

AFFIRMATIONS

Add these affirmations to your daily list, all taken from the Bible:

"I have been chosen by God."

"I am a beloved child of God."

"I am the righteousness of God in Christ."

"I am blessed."

"I am a whole person through Christ."

"I have been delivered from the hand of the enemy."

"I am prospering for the sake of the Gospel."

"I am healed."

"I am a strong and positive person."

"My God will never leave me nor forsake me."

. . . And the list is endless. Build your own!

CHAPTER 14

THE UNAPPRECIATED

And now I give you the greatest words that my church congregation hears each time I speak: "IN CLOSING." (I'm allowed four of those!)

You won't find many in the work force today who actually feel appreciated. John Q. Public can be extremely coldhearted and very mean-spirited. Can you imagine trying to make out a list of those who feel unappreciated? The list would be endless.

How many moms have told their disrespectful children (or husbands) through tears, "I've been in the kitchen slaving over this hot stove all day, and THIS is the thanks I get?" How about a coach in any sport? You love them when they're winning, but you hate them when they're losing (or not playing your kid). A teacher is loved when a student is passing, but not so much when the student is struggling.

It seems law enforcement is disrespected and often hated when they make an arrest or write out that speeding (unjust) ticket, but they are loved and respected when running into harm's way to risk their lives to save someone else's. I could go on and on with my list of the unappreciated, but I would probably leave your job off and be in trouble.

Self-importance is a vital part of our makeup. It's like the man who requested prayer in his church for his pending **major** surgery. The curious prayer warriors asked him, "What major surgery are you having?" He said, "Toe surgery." A sweet sister replied, "Excuse me, Brother, but toe surgery is NOT major surgery." He said, "It is if it's YOUR toe."

It's only natural for anyone who is giving it their best on the job to have the need for some appreciation and recognition for their hard work. I mentioned earlier that people will normally go where they are celebrated, not where they are tolerated. When there is lack of appreciation, it will make for a difficult workplace.

Note: That truly was the original intent of this book. I wanted to celebrate the "unappreciated." In doing that, I began to think about, *"Who might possibly be the most unappreciated person who ever lived?"* (I'm not considering you on this one! LOL!)

UH, OH! TIME TO GET PREACHY! (DON'T BE AFRAID. I DO THIS A LOT!) PLEASE CONTINUE TO READ, ESPECIALLY IF YOU ARE NOT ALL THAT RELIGIOUS OR "CHURCHY." IT MAY NOT BE WHAT YOU THINK!

Being raised in a pastor's home gave me the opportunity to hear the message of Christianity on a regular basis. I was born on a Tuesday, was in church the next Sunday, and did not miss a single Sunday, Wednesday, or special revival service until I was twelve years of age. My parents believed in going to church, and if the door was open, we were there (like it or not). I had a ringside seat to watch "church" in action. I honestly loved most of it, especially the music!

My parents were the kindest and most loving pastors that I have ever met. I was fortunate enough to see some real, genuine "love of God" on display. Taking care of the hurting, the lonely, feeding the hungry, clothing the naked, comforting the broken, and seeing lives totally transformed was a common occurrence.

Of course, I got to see the bad side of church as well. I witnessed the backbiting, hypocrisy, condemnation, judging, and the proverbial "casting of stones." Even though I witnessed those negatives, my heart seemed to be established with such a deep love for God and the "Gospel" that my faith could not be shaken.

By the age of eight, God had touched my heart in such a unique and profound way that I knew one day Christian ministry, in whatever capacity, would be my life. Even as I grew into my teens, that "call" never left me.

CHALLENGES

As I grew in years and in my faith, several questions and challenges also grew. I never considered myself a rebel, but I always seemed to struggle with a lot of the man-made, churchy stuff. Countless denominations and numerous and varied sects of the church always puzzled me. The spirit of competition producing bitter rivalries between church groups surely could not have been the original intent of our Heavenly Father. The pride, arrogance, and boasting from each group with a "we're right and you're wrong" (even to the point of exclusion) attitude, has always been quite nauseating to me.

Note: One thing I do believe I have figured out. When we get to heaven, we're all going to sadly discover, WE WERE ALL WRONG (about something). LOL!

RELIGION HAS A PROBLEM WITH "GRACE"

The sports world, business world, educational world, etc. are all performance based. And, of course, that's okay. This book has a sports theme. Those familiar with that world know this: If you perform well, you play; if you don't perform well, you will find a place on the bench. If you work hard in the business world, you get promoted or get raises and bonuses. If you perform poorly, you get fired. Perform well in school or you fail. Success in life is built on the power of mankind's ability to perform at a very high standard.

Religion can be quite complicated. Unfortunately, it too is all built on man's ability to perform well. Self-performance, self-effort, self-discipline, etc. are entwined throughout the figure of every man's religion. Every religion on the earth has a built-in system of man faithfully executing certain rites, rituals, acts, indulgences, deeds, kindnesses, sacrifices, etc. to merit some kind of favor or to avert a particular wrath, judgment, or punishment. Religion carries with it some heavy duty pressure on the performer. It leaves with it a human "blood trail" of a "self-based" mentality.

The Old Testament in the Bible is filled with such practices. The arrogance of man boasting that he could do anything God commanded him to do led God to establish over 600 laws for man to perfectly perform in order to earn His favor. You've probably heard of "The Big 10."

This practice completely went against the original intent of the heart of God who never wanted to "force" man into submission with vicious threats of judgment.

God's heart is, and always has been, love. Man's arrogant, proud, and haughty spirit has always been the disruptive force to the plan of God.

LAW VS. GRACE

"For the LAW was given by Moses, but GRACE and TRUTH came by Jesus Christ" (John 1:17).

The Bible is divided into two parts – the Old Testament and the New Testament. Understanding the difference in these two covenants will be the difference maker in mankind's life of peace, joy, power, health, success, love, confidence with God, etc. or a life of frustration, lack, weakness, uncertainty, grief, sickness, emotional instability, condemnation, shame, etc.

"Study to shew thyself approved unto God, a workman that needeth not to be ashamed, rightly dividing the word of truth" (2 Timothy 2:15).

Christianity has not done a very good job of rightly dividing. It would be impossible for me to do an exhaustive presentation of this subject, but let me hit some highlights.

THE PURPOSE OF MAN'S BEST EFFORT

"Wherefore the law is holy, and the commandment holy, and just, and good" (Romans 7:12).

Sounds good. Right? There was just one problem. Man couldn't keep the law. Not many have ever been told that. Most people have been beaten to death spiritually with a rod of condemnation, fear, shame, correction, and judgment. Most church services have been reduced to an hour or so of being "bawled out in public." Many times we leave a church meeting with a "greater load or burden" coming out than we had going in.

Pulpits have become thrones of shame, condemnation, and judgment rather than a place of invitation to discover the grace (favor), love, and mercy of God. A constant barrage of hearing about what we should be, could be, ought to be, need to try to be, or hopefully someday gonna be, is what we get. And, God's gonna getcha if you don't straighten up. We don't often hear the truth about what we "be." Never "measuring up" has now become the theme of the Church.

Religion screams, "Do more." You've heard it. You've got to pray more, love more, give more, read your Bible more, go to church more, and on and on it goes. It has a harsh condemning cry of "You haven't done enough." (Note: I personally always wondered, "How do I know when I've done enough?")

Several years ago I met a friend of mine going down the street who at one time was a regular church attendee. I expressed that we had missed him. His reason for not coming back to church deeply disturbed me. He said, "Pastor Marlon, I honestly do love the Lord, and I wanted to be a good Christian. I JUST COULDN'T DO IT!"

He couldn't DO IT? What was that supposed to mean? I realized then that I had been making Christianity all about what you DO and not about who you ARE! When a man finds out "who he is," it will affect what he does. More on that later!

We must understand the purpose of the law in order to see where God was going with this thing. According to the Apostle Paul, it's exactly the opposite of what most people think. Check out these verses of Scripture from Romans 3:19-20:

The law was given to those who were **"under the law: (so) that every mouth may be stopped, and all the world may become guilty before God.**

"Therefore by the deeds (works) **of the law there shall no flesh be justified** (made right before God) **in his sight: for by the law is the knowledge of sin."**

The Jews of that day were saying, and it is what many today are saying, "You have got to keep every one of the Old Testament laws. God will judge you based upon how well you 'perform' and whether you have been perfectly obedient to the laws of God." That couldn't be further from the truth. The law was given to take away man's ability to boast and strip man of his excuses.

Some still had a tendency to boast, thinking that God grades lawbreakers on a "curve." "I've kept most of the law." "I've kept eight of the Ten Commandments." BUSTED! James 2:10 says, **"For whosoever shall keep the WHOLE law, and yet offend in ONE point, he is guilty of all."** The demands of the law were brutal. If you mowed your grass on a Sabbath day, you were just as guilty as the man who committed adultery or murder. OUCH! That's not fair. It wasn't intended to be.

The law (as previously mentioned) was holy, just, and good. The problem is, it was never intended to make man holy, just, and good. The law wasn't given to show us the goodness of God. It was given to reveal to man his weakness and sin. Every time man heard or saw the Ten Commandments, he would have a sense of guilt, sin, or shame. It was given to bring man to the end of his performance mentality and break him down to the point he realized that he needed a Savior. Man, even through all of his good efforts and kind deeds, could never save himself. It would take the efforts of another – JESUS.

The Apostle Paul takes this law thing a step further when he says in 2 Corinthians 3:6-7: We are **"ministers of the new testament; not of the letter** (law) **. . . for the letter** (law) **killeth, but the spirit giveth life. But if the ministration**

of death, written and engraven in stones. . . ." Check out verse 9: **"For if the ministration of condemnation. . . ."** (If we are to be ministers of the New, then why do we seem to major on the Old?)

Are you getting this? Paul called the Ten Commandments *the ministry of death* and *the ministry of condemnation.* In the Book of Exodus when Moses came down from the mountain with the Ten Commandments, that day 3,000 people died. They had built a golden calf to worship instead of worshiping God. One was, **"Thou shalt have no other gods before me"** (Exodus 20:3). They did and they died.

Let's sum up this part. The law was based on a system of "do good, get good"/"do bad, get bad." If man kept the laws of God, he was blessed. If man failed to keep ALL the laws of God perfectly, he would experience the wrath and judgment of God sent to punish the "lawbreaker." That's religion.

What about you? Have you TRIED to gain the favor of God through your doing good, or maybe your "looking good"? You have set yourself up for disappointment. The majority of the church today looks like they have been baptized in lemon juice! Bitter, sour, mad at the world, unfulfilled, and empty. Why? The law (man's best effort to please God) will always keep a man dissatisfied by design.

HERE COMES JESUS TO THE RESCUE

Remember John 1:17 **"The law was given by Moses, BUT grace and truth came by Jesus Christ."**

God saw the condition of His man. No matter how much man tried to impress God by his self-performing, self-righteous spirit, he was always coming up frustrated and empty. That's why Jesus stood in the middle of those heavily oppressed by the law and declared:

> **"Come to Me, all you who labor** (working to gain favor with God) **and are heavy-laden and overburdened** (by religion)**, and I will cause you to rest. [I will ease and relieve and refresh your souls.]**
> **"Take My yoke upon you and learn of Me, for I am gentle (meek) and humble (lowly) in heart, and you will find rest (relief and ease and refreshment and recreation and blessed quiet) for your souls."**
> **Matthew 11:28-29** AMP

That doesn't sound like a lot of the Christian experiences that I am familiar with. Most are not resting in the assurance that Jesus came to provide, but are struggling in their confidence as a Christian. They are still trying to "do" to become.

Note: Let me say this about grace. Grace is not a doctrine, a message, or a movement. Grace is a Person. His name is Jesus. He personally has provided rest and confidence for the believing one.

God placed Jesus smack in the middle of a religious people bound by the legalistic prison of self-performance. His ministry would be showing people that a NEW and LIVING system was on the way and was actually here now, standing before them. They didn't get it. They totally rejected Him. They fought for their right to be imprisoned.

Most people today, even church people, have no idea that through the grace of God (His undeserved favor) the prison doors have been opened. Mankind now has access to God, not based upon what he does or doesn't do, but based upon what Jesus did through His death, burial, and resurrection.

Because of man's tradition and his inability to step outside the religious box, he sits inside the prison cell with abundant life beckoning him to come out. Man has the ability today to come before God without the sense of sin, guilt, condemnation, inferiority, or shame. Why? Because Jesus took it all upon Himself on the cross.

What about wrath and judgment coming upon all of us because of our sin? GOOD NEWS! Jesus bore it in His own body on the tree. Doesn't sin have to be punished? It was! All of the wrath, judgment, and condemnation for our sin were placed upon Jesus. He bore it all! Our debt was paid in full because of Jesus. That's GOOD NEWS!

DOING VS. BELIEVING

There seems to be a force on the inside of every person that craves to be rewarded for the good they have done. Trophies, rings, medals, ribbons, plaques, certificates, etc. are accepted with great pride, all thanks for a job well done.

Heaven is not a reward for all the good things you have done. Are you shocked by that statement? There will be a reward system there, but a person's entrance into heaven itself is not one of them. If it were a reward, then man could "boast" about how he got there. Clearly the Apostle Paul, the Apostle of grace, said to the church at Ephesus:

> **"For by GRACE** *(undeserved, unmerited, unearned FAVOR)* **are ye saved through faith; and that not of YOURSELVES: it is the GIFT** *(not a reward)* **of God:**
>
> **"Not of WORKS, lest any man should BOAST."**
> **Ephesians 2:8-9**

No man will be able to say, "I did _____. That's why I'm in heaven." You will be there because you accepted God's GIFT of life in the person of His Son, Jesus Christ.

The Old was a "doing" system. The New is a "believing" system. What about proper behavior? Shouldn't we act right? Of course! But God now has placed greater confidence in man's "believing" than He has in man's "doing." God believes that if a person "believes right," they will "act right."

Jesus taught in His earth walk under the legalistic system of the law. He would confront that law with every opportunity. When He gave the woman who was caught in the very act of adultery the gift of "no condemnation," it infuriated her religious accusers. They wanted her judged according to the law, which was death by stoning.

Grace (Jesus) will never take part as an accusing voice against you. He has made love, forgiveness, and mercy available to every person. He is not the condemner. Satan's very title is "accuser of the brethren." It is his accusing voice that continually says, "You haven't done enough, or you need to do more to be made right (or stay right) with God. Grace says, "You have been made right because of what Jesus did. Believe it."

Most people have heard John 3:16: **"For God so loved the world, that he gave his only begotten Son, that whosoever BELIEVETH in him should not perish, but have everlasting life."** But what about John 3:17: **"For God sent not his Son into the world to condemn the world;**

but that the world through him might be saved." All He asks is that we believe it and receive it BY FAITH!

Under the OLD, repentance led to the goodness of God. Under the NEW, it is the goodness of God that leads a person to repentance.

In two specific places in the Bible, someone asked, "What must we do to be saved or to inherit eternal life?" We see two different answers from two different dispensations – LAW and GRACE.

In Matthew 19:16-22, Jesus said to the rich young ruler, who was under the law, **"Keep** (do all) **the commandments"** (v. 17). The young man said, "I have." Jesus said, "You still lack one thing." That's what trying to merit the favor of God through self-performance will do. It always leaves you lacking. (I encourage you to read the total account for yourself.)

Then in Acts 16:16-31, we find Paul and Silas in jail for preaching the Gospel of grace. This was after the death, burial, and resurrection of Jesus. At midnight Paul and Silas prayed and sang praises to God. As a result, God literally shook the prison house and freed them and all of the other prisoners. (This is the original version of "jailhouse rock"!)

The jailer was about to take his own life out of fear, but Paul and Silas intervened and told him that no one had fled. Then the jailer asked, **"What must I do to be saved?"** (v. 30). Paul said, **"BELIEVE on the Lord Jesus Christ, and thou shalt be saved, and thy house"** (v. 31). (Again, I encourage you to read the entire account for yourself.)

Notice the difference in these two accounts? One response under the Old was, "DO THIS." A completely different response under the New is, "BELIEVE THIS."

CHRISTIANITY IS NOT RELIGION

As I close, I want to say this: I HATE RELIGION! It will destroy your life. I have seen it destroy many. Religion knocked down our Twin Towers in New York City and killed thousands of our brothers and sisters. Those murderers were looking for a "reward."

Religion will depict God as an overbearing ogre placing unmeetable demands upon His children. Christianity, on the other hand, reveals a loving, compassionate Heavenly Father who came looking for us when sin caused us to be separated from Him.

Which do you prefer? More confidence in what you have done for God, or more confidence in what God, through Christ, has done for you? There is nothing you will ever do that could make Him love you more and nothing you will ever do that could make Him love you less. GOD LOVES YOU! God proved it by giving us Jesus.

ONE LAST THOUGHT

One last thought about this sports officiating thing. The best sports officials I have ever seen at one time or another STINK!

Your Invitation to Accept Jesus Christ as Lord and Savior

I invite you today to make Jesus Christ the Lord of your life, and then allow His Holy Spirit to help you live your life to the glory of God. I'm not where I want to be, but thank God, through Christ I am not where I used to be. I am a work in progress as well as the rest of the Christian world. It has been quite a journey.

First John 4:19 says, **"We love him, because he first loved us."**

Romans 5:17 says, **"They which receive abundance of GRACE and of the gift of RIGHTEOUSNESS shall reign in life by one, Jesus Christ."**

Second Corinthians 5:17 states, **"Therefore if any man BE in Christ, he is a NEW CREATURE: old things are passed away; behold, all things are become new."**

CHRISTIANITY IS NOT WHAT YOU DO; IT'S WHAT YOU BE (through faith in Jesus Christ)!

Knowledge about what you BE (are) will always affect what you do (with the assuring thought that you will never be perfect or good enough to earn any of God's goodness). Confidence in the fact that He has made you righteous by faith is the ROOT! Your actions are the fruit!

How do you know that you are right before God? YOU BELIEVE YOU ARE! Faith (believing) is your confidence!

PRAYER

Father, I come to You now in the name of Jesus. I, like Marlon, want to leave religion and step into true Christianity.

I ask You to forgive me for doing my own thing my own way. I believe that Jesus is Your Son, Father, and that He died for my sins and was raised from the dead.

I accept You, Jesus, as my personal Lord and Savior. Thank You for empowering me with the Holy Spirit so that I am equipped to live an overcoming and abundant life.

I submit to Your lordship, Jesus, and I thank You for new life today! Amen.

For Information Booking Contact:

Marlon Sparks
P.O. Box 692
Perryton, TX 79070
marlongsparks20@gmail.com
806-228-0117

www.ingramcontent.com/pod-product-compliance
Lightning Source LLC
LaVergne TN
LVHW021552080426
835510LV00019B/2479